Untold Power of Productivity To Achieve More Mini Productivity Book

Reliable Growth Partner

ISBN 978-93-5667-463-9
© Reliable Growth Partner 2023
Published in India 2023 by Pencil

A brand of
One Point Six Technologies Pvt. Ltd.
123, Building J2, Shram Seva Premises,
Wadala Truck Terminal, Wadala (E)
Mumbai 400037, Maharashtra, INDIA
E connect@thepencilapp.com
W www.thepencilapp.com

Author biography

A ***reliable growth partner*** is one among you who is growth chasers in life. The ultimate aim this partner is to grow together while chasing his growth and improving his life forward. He would like to be a secret weapon, who bring expertise, resources, and a fresh perspective to the table, propelling one towards their goals and helping them reach new levels of prosperity. He wish to share a unique blend of wisdom, experience,and determination, helping one to achieve their aspirations and reach their full potential, step by step. This partner is one who is also facing various challenges who can overcome obstacles and navigate challenges, as well as take advantage of new opportunities. A reliable growth partner can bring a fresh perspective, new ideas, that can help drive your personal growth. Additionally, having a reliable growth partner can provide a sense of understanding and stability, allowing a company or individual to focus on their goals and work towards their vision.

CONTENTS

Contents

Regular Exercise And Physical Activity
Chapter 7: Staying On Track
Setting Measurable Goals And Tracking Progress
Celebrating Success
Adjusting And Refining Techniques For Continued Improvement
Chapter 8: Conclusion
- The benefits of productivity
- Moving forward with purpose and drive
- Embracing a growth mindset and continuous learning.
The book offers practical and easy-to-implement tips and tricks for increasing productivity and achieving more in less time. By following the methods outlined in the book, **readers can improve their time management skills, boost their focus and concentration,**
and ultimately reach their goals faster and more effectively.
Hope You Will Like This Book !

Introduction To Productivity

Understanding the importance of productivity

Productivity is important as it measures the efficiency of converting inputs, such as **time, effort and resources,**into outputs or desired results. Increased productivity can lead to higher economic growth, improved competitiveness, and higher living standards. It can also help individuals to manage **their time more effectively and achieve their goals more efficiently.**By focusing on productivity, individuals and organizations can improve their performance and increase their success. Productivity is a crucial aspect of both personal and organizational success. It refers to the ability to efficiently use available resources, such as **time, effort, and materials, to produce desired results**. High productivity means that more can be achieved in less time, leading to greater output and efficiency. By understanding the importance of productivity and taking steps to improve it, individuals and organizations can work smarter, not harder, and achieve their goals more effectively. Whether in the workplace, at home, or in other areas of life, a focus on productivity can lead to **greater success and satisfaction.**

Setting Goals And Defining Success

Goal setting and success definition are two crucial elements in **personal and professional growth and development**. By clearly defining what you **want to achieve and what constitutes success for those goals**, you can focus your efforts and make steady progress towards your desired outcomes. Whether you're pursuing personal or professional goals, having a clear understanding of what you want to accomplish and what success means to you is essential for **creating a roadmap to your success and maintaining motivation along the way**. Setting goals is the process of defining what you want to achieve, while defining success is determining what outcomes or accomplishments represent success for those goals. It's important to set **specific, measurable, achievable, relevant, and time-bound (SMART) goals**and regularly assess your progress towards them to maintain motivation and adjust as necessary. It's also important to have a clear definition of success that aligns with your **values and priorities, and to celebrate your successes**along the way. Here is an example story to illustrate the concepts of goal setting and defining success:

Meet Jane, a recent college graduate who has just started her first job as a marketing coordinator. She's eager to make a positive impact in her new role and grow in her career. To do this, Jane knows she needs to set goals and define success for herself. So, she takes some time to **reflect on her skills, interests, and what she wants to achieve in the next 5 years**. *She realizes that she wants to become* **a marketing manager***and eventually start her own marketing agency. With her career aspirations in mind, Jane sets the following goals: Learn about all* **aspects of marketing by attending industry conferences and workshops, and**

by completing online courses.*Develop her leadership skills by taking on additional responsibilities within her team and volunteering for projects outside her comfort zone. Build a strong professional network by participating in industry events and connecting with others in her field on LinkedIn. For each of these goals, Jane defines success as follows: Success for her learning goal is attending* **at least two conferences and workshops, completing two online courses,***and being able to* **apply what she's learned to her work.****Success for her leadership goal is being recognized for her contributions to her team and successfully leading at least one project. Success for her networking goal is having a* **minimum of 100 connections on LinkedIn***and being able to call upon her network for advice and opportunities.****With her goals and definitions of success in place, Jane can now focus on taking concrete steps towards achieving them. By regularly reviewing her progress and adjusting as needed, she can stay on track and celebrate her success along the way.*

Identifying Time-Wasters And Distractions

We all in our life at some point of time try to manage time, but in reality **time flows away like waves at the seashore.** Time wasters are activities or habits that consume our time without providing any meaningful results or contribution to our goals. These distractions can come in many forms, including **technology, repetitive tasks, procrastination, and others.**By identifying and eliminating time wasters, we can increase our productivity and focus on what truly matters. In this process, it is important to be honest with ourselves and evaluate our habits and behaviors in order to create a more efficient and fulfilling use of our time. Identifying time wasters is a critical step in maximizing your productivity and achieving your goals. Whether it's procrastination, excessive social media use, unproductive meetings, or disorganized tasks, these habits can significantly impact the way you allocate your time. To effectively manage your time, it is crucial to recognize what activities are taking up your time and energy, without contributing to your overall objectives. By examining your daily routines and patterns, you can **determine what changes need to be made to increase your efficiency and reduce the amount of time wasted.**Additionally, implementing good time management strategies such as prioritizing tasks, streamlining processes, and delegating responsibilities can help you to stay focused and avoid distractions. By identifying and addressing time wasters, you **can create more space in your schedule**for the things that matter most and ultimately achieve more success.

To identify time wasters and distractions, you can follow these steps.

Track your time : Keep a log of how you spend your time for a few days to see where most of it goes.

Identify patterns : Look for repetitive activities that take up a lot of your time but don't seem to lead to meaningful results.

Evaluate your habits : Consider if there are habits or behaviors you have that are **taking away**from your productivity.

Assess To Techonology : Technology can be a major source of distraction, particularly social media and other leisure websites.

Set boundaries : Establish clear boundaries for **how you use your time and make a plan to limit distractions**.

By doing this, you can be more aware of where your time is going and make changes to increase your productivity. Here is an example story of identifying time wasters could be as follows

Sophia , a project manager at a tech company, noticed that her team was consistently **missing deadlines and delivering subpar work.***She decided to investigate the issue and keep track of how each team member was spending their time during work hours. After a week of monitoring she discovered that a few team members were* **spending several hours each day***browsing social media, playing online games, and engaging in personal conversations.*
These activities were taking up valuable time that should have been dedicated to work tasks. Sophia scheduled a meeting with the team and presented her findings. She made it clear that while **taking short breaks during the workday was acceptable,***extended periods of time dedicated to non-work activities was unacceptable and would not be tolerated. She also implemented tools and systems to help the team stay focused and productive, such as* **time tracking software and regular check-ins***with team members to monitor their progress. As a result of these changes, the team was able to meet deadlines and deliver high-quality work. Sophia efforts to identify and* **address time wasters helped to create a more productive and efficient team***, and ensured that the company was using its resources to their fullest potential.*

Mastering Time Management

Prioritizing tasks

Prioritizing tasks refers to the process of evaluating the **importance and urgency of different tasks**and arranging them in a way that optimizes time and resources. This helps individuals and teams to focus on the most important tasks first, leading to increased efficiency, productivity, and success. There are various methods for prioritizing tasks, for example **Eisenhower Matrix,**which categorizes tasks based on urgency and importance, and the **ABC method,**which assigns a priority level based on the potential impact of a task. Regardless of the method used, prioritizing tasks requires clear goal-setting, effective time management, and regular reassessment of priorities to ensure that tasks align with changing circumstances and priorities.By prioritizing tasks, individuals and teams can ensure that they are making the most of their time and resources, and are **able to focus on what is truly important in achieving their goals.** Additionally, prioritizing tasks can also help individuals and teams to reduce stress and improve their work-life balance. When tasks are prioritized, individuals are able to **manage their workload in a more organized and manageable way,**allowing them to avoid feeling overwhelmed and burned out.   By focusing on the most important tasks first, individuals can also be more confident in their decision-making and feel a greater sense of control over their workload.Moreover, prioritizing tasks can also help individuals and teams to improve their accountability and achieve better results. When tasks are assigned a priority level, individuals are **more likely to take ownership of their responsibilities**and follow through with **their commitments, leading to improved results and a sense of accomplishment**. In conclusion, prioritizing tasks is a valuable skill that can help individuals and teams to be more productive, efficient, and successful in their work and personal lives. Common let's understand this with John's Life. *John was a busy sales manager at a growing company. He had a lot on his plate and was feeling overwhelmed by his workload. He was struggling to keep up with all of his responsibilities and was consistently missing deadlines.One day, John realized that he needed to change his approach to managing his tasks. He decided to prioritize his tasks using the Eisenhower Matrix, which categorizes tasks based on their urgency and importance.John spent a few hours going through his to-do list and categorizing each task into one of four categories:* **urgent and important, important but not urgent, urgent but not important, and neither urgent nor important.***Next, John tackled the tasks that were both urgent and important, such as meeting with clients and responding to urgent emails. He then moved on to the important but not urgent tasks, such as planning and strategizing for the next quarter.By prioritizing his tasks, John was able to focus on* **what was truly important and avoid getting bogged down by less important tasks**. *As a result, he was able to be more productive, meet deadlines, and deliver better results.John's experience shows the importance of prioritizing tasks and how it can help individuals to manage their workload, be more productive, and* *achieve their goals.*

Using To-Do Lists And Calendars

Using to-do lists is a simple but effective way to prioritize tasks and manage one's workload. A to-do list is a list of tasks that need to be completed, arranged in order of priority. It allows individuals to keep track of their responsibilities, stay organized, and avoid forgetting important tasks. To effectively use a to-do list, **one should regularly update it with new tasks and rearrange them based on changing priorities.**It is also helpful to break down large tasks into smaller, more manageable ones and to prioritize them accordingly. To-do lists can be created using a variety of methods, including pen and paper, spreadsheet programs, or task management apps. Some people prefer to use physical to-do lists as they can be more satisfying to cross off, while others prefer digital lists as they can be accessed and updated more easily. In addition to helping individuals manage their workload, to-do lists can also help to improve productivity and reduce stress. By providing a clear and organized overview of one's responsibilities, to-do lists allow individuals to focus on what is truly important and avoid feeling overwhelmed. In conclusion, using to-do lists is a **simple and effective way to prioritize tasks and manage one's workload**. Whether one uses a physical or digital list, taking the time to create and maintain a to-do list can help to improve productivity, reduce stress, and achieve one's goals. Using both a to-do list and a calendar is a powerful combination for prioritizing tasks and managing one's workload.

A to-do list provides a comprehensive overview of all the tasks that need to be completed, while a calendar provides a visual representation of deadlines and appointments.To effectively use a to-do list and a calendar, one should regularly update both with new tasks and deadlines, and rearrange tasks on the to-do list based on changing priorities. It is also **helpful to color-code appointments and tasks on the calendar to quickly see**which are the most important or time-sensitive.When using both a to-do list and a calendar, it is important to review both regularly to ensure that tasks are aligned with changing circumstances and priorities. By doing this, individuals can avoid overcommitting and ensure that they are focusing on what is truly important.

Common let's understand *How To Do List impacted Sara's Lifestyle Positively ?*

*Sara was a busy freelance copywriter. She had a lot of projects and deadlines to keep track of, and was feeling overwhelmed by her workload. She often found herself forgetting important tasks or missing deadlines.One day, Sara decided to start using a **to-do list to manage her tasks and prioritize her workload.**She spent a few hours creating a comprehensive list of all her tasks, and arranged them in order of priority.Each day, Sara would start by reviewing her to-do list and deciding which tasks were the most important to focus on. She found that having a clear and organized overview of her tasks made **it easier for her to stay on track and avoid feeling overwhelmed**. Sara also found that using a to-do list helped her to be more productive and efficient. By focusing on the most important tasks first, she was able to **complete more in a shorter amount of time and meet all of her deadlines.** Sara's experience shows the power of using a to-do list to prioritize tasks and manage one's workload. Whether you're a* *freelancer, student, or busy professional, a to-do list can help you stay organized and achieve your goals.*

Time Blocking and Batch Processing

Time blocking and batch processing are two effective techniques for **managing time and prioritizing tasks**. Time blocking is a method of scheduling specific blocks of time for specific tasks. This allows individuals to focus on one task at a time and avoid distractions, leading to increased productivity and efficiency. For example, one could block out the **first two hours**of the day for answering emails, the **next three hours for working on a project**, and so on.

Time blocking is a technique that involves dividing your day into designated time slots and assigning specific activities or tasks to each slot. This methodhelps to **prioritize tasks, increase focus, and boost productivity by reducing distractions and providing structure to your day.** By scheduling your time in advance, you can ensure that you have dedicated time for important tasks and avoid feeling overwhelmed. This technique can be done using a variety of tools, including paper planners, digital calendars, or simple to-do lists. The key to successful time blocking is **consistency and flexibility**to adjust your schedule as needed.

Let's take the example of a busy professional named Serena who used to feel overwhelmed with her workload and was constantly struggling to complete all of her tasks in a day. She would often find herself multitasking, which led to decreased focus and reduced productivity.One day, Serena decided to try time blocking. She started by mapping out her typical workday and identifying the tasks that needed to be completed.She then divided her day into specific time slots, assigning a task to each slot. For example, from 9 am to 11 am she dedicated to responding to emails, from 11 am to 12 pm was for a meeting, from 1 pm to 3 pm was for project work, and so on.Serena found that time blocking helped her to focus on one task at a time, which increased her productivity. She was able to complete her tasks on time and had a clearer sense of control over her day. By following a structured schedule, she was able to reduce stress and felt more organized.Over time, Serena found that time blocking was a valuable tool in her time management arsenal and helped her to achieve a better work-life balance.She was able to prioritize tasks, allocate sufficient time for each task, and avoid feeling overwhelmed. Serena highly recommends time blocking to anyone looking to increase their productivity and manage their time more effectively.

Batch processing,on the other hand, is a method of grouping similar tasks together and working on them in one batch, rather than scattering them throughout the day. This helps to **minimize distractions, reduce the time spent switching between tasks, and increase overall productivity.**For example, instead of answering emails as they come in, one could block out a specific time of the day to answer all emails in one batch.Using both time blocking and batch processing can help individuals prioritize tasks, manage their time more efficiently, and reduce stress. By focusing on one task at a time and minimizing distractions, individuals can increase their productivity and achieve their goals.In conclusion, time blocking and batch processing are two effective techniques for managing time and prioritizing tasks. By using these techniques, individuals can increase their productivity, reduce stress, and achieve their goals.

Let's take the example of a small business owner named John. John used to handle all the tasks of his business, from managing finances to customer service, on his own. This resulted in long working hours, burnout, and decreased efficiency. John then discovered batch processing and decided to give it a try. He grouped similar tasks together and completed them in batches, instead of handling them one by one. For example, he would dedicate Monday mornings to answering customer emails, Wednesday afternoons to processing invoices, and Friday mornings to following up with clients. By using batch processing,

John was able to increase his efficiency and reduce the time spent on repetitive tasks. He found that he was able to complete his work faster and with higher accuracy.*John also noticed that batch processing allowed him to stay organized and prioritize his tasks more effectively. In the end, batch processing became an integral part of John's business operations. It helped him to manage his workload, reduce stress, and increase his overall*

productivity. John now recommends batch processing to other small business owners looking to streamline their operations and improve their time management skills.

Overcoming Procrastination

Understanding Why We Procrastinate

Procrastination is the act of delaying or postponing tasks, despite knowing that they need to be completed. It can be a result of various factors, including fear of failure, lack of motivation, distractions, or poor time management skills. Procrastination can have a negative impact on personal and professional life, as it leads to decreased productivity, increased stress, and a feeling of being overwhelmed. It's a common issue that affects many people, but it's possible to overcome with the right strategies and mindset. To overcome procrastination, it's important to identify the **root cause, set clear goals, break tasks into smaller and manageable parts, eliminate distractions, and establish a routine.**By implementing these strategies, individuals can overcome procrastination and achieve their goals effectively.

Let's understand this with the Story of Selena Meet Selena, a college student who has always struggled with procrastination. Despite having the best of intentions, Selena would often find herself delaying her assignments until the last minute. This resulted in staying up late, feeling stressed, and turning in subpar work. One day, Selena decided to seek help and understand why she procrastinated. After some reflection and research, she discovered that her procrastination was driven by a fear of failure. She was afraid that she wouldn't be able to complete her assignments to her high standards, so she put them off.With this newfound understanding, Selena set out to overcome her procrastination. She started by breaking her assignments into smaller and manageable parts. She also established a routine where she dedicated specific times of the day to complete her work, and eliminated all distractions, including social media and her phone.Selena also found that setting clear goals and positive self-talk helped her stay motivated and focused on her tasks. Over time, Selena was able to **overcome her procrastination and turn in high-quality work on time**. *In the end, Selena learned that understanding the root cause of her procrastination was the key to overcoming it. By implementing the right strategies and mindset, she was able to improve her productivity, reduce stress, and achieve her goals effectively.*

Implementing Techniques For Staying Motivated

Here are some techniques that can help overcome procrastination

Identify the root cause :Understanding why you procrastinate is the first step in overcoming it. Identify the underlying reasons and address them directly.

Set clear goals :Set realistic and specific goals for the tasks you need to complete. Writing them down can help make them more concrete.Break tasks into smaller parts : Breaking down a large task into smaller, manageable parts can make it feel less overwhelming and easier to start.

Use a to-do list :Prioritize your tasks and use a to-do list to track your progress. This can help you stay organized and focused.Eliminate distractions : Minimize distractions such as social media, email, or your phone while working.

Establish a routine :Set aside dedicated time each day to work on your tasks and stick to a routine.

Use positive self-talk :Encourage yourself with positive self-talk and acknowledge your achievements, no matter how small.

Reward yourself :Celebrate your accomplishments and reward yourself for a job well done. This can help maintain motivation and a positive attitude.By implementing these techniques, you can overcome procrastination, increase productivity, and achieve your goals effectively. Remember that overcoming procrastination is a process and it takes time and practice to make it a habit. Keep working on it and don't be discouraged by setbacks.

Staying Focused And Avoiding Distractions

Staying focused and avoiding distractions is crucial for productivity and success. Distractions can easily disrupt your workflow and take away valuable time and energy from your tasks. To stay focused, it's important to create an environment that supports concentration and minimizes distractions. Here are some tips to help you stay focused and avoid distractions

Eliminate Distractions :Minimize distractions such as social media, email, or your phone while working.

Create a Dedicated Workspace :Set up a workspace that is comfortable and conducive to concentration.

Set Clear Goals :Set specific and realistic goals for your tasks, and break them down into smaller parts.

Use A To-Do List: Keep track of your tasks and prioritize them using a to-do list. This helps you stay organized and focused.

Establish A Routine :Dedicate specific times of the day to complete your work, and stick to a routine.

Take Frequent Breaks :Regular breaks can help you avoid burnout and maintain focus over time.

Avoid Multitasking :Focusing on one task at a time is more effective than multitasking.

By following these tips, you can avoid distractions and stay focused on your tasks, which can lead to increased productivity and success.

Remember to be gentle with yourself and don't get discouraged if you get sidetracked. Just get back on track and keep moving forward.

Enhancing Focus And Concentration

Here are some tips to **enhance focus and concentration and minimize distractions :**

Eliminate distractions : Turn off notifications on your phone, close unnecessary tabs on your computer, and create a quiet workspace to minimize distractions.

Use the Pomodoro Technique : This technique involves working in focused 25-minute increments, followed by a short break.

Exercise regularly : Exercise has been shown to improve focus and concentration, so try to incorporate physical activity into your routine.

Get adequate sleep : Lack of sleep can negatively affect focus and concentration, so make sure to get enough restful sleep each night.

Take breaks : Regular breaks can help you avoid burnout and refresh your mind, leading to improved focus and concentration.

Stay organized : Keep a clear and organized workspace, prioritize tasks, and use a to-do list to keep track of your progress.

Use mindfulness techniques: Mindfulness and meditation can help you stay focused and calm, even in stressful situations.

Limit caffeine and sugar intake: Consuming too much caffeine or sugar can lead to jitters, anxiety, and decreased focus.

By following these tips, you can enhance your focus and concentration and minimize distractions, leading to increased productivity and success. Remember that developing good habits takes time and practice, so be patient and persistent

Let's Understand This Using Jacob' Story

Jacob is a software developer who is finding it difficult to concentrate on his work. He often gets distracted by **notifications from his phone and other interruptions**. *He decides that he needs to improve his focus and concentration to be more productive and meet his deadlines. John starts by creating a dedicated workspace for himself. He* **declutters his desk and eliminates any distractions, such as turning off notifications on his phone and closing unnecessary tabs on his computer.***He also starts incorporating mindfulness and meditation practices into his daily routine to help him stay calm and focused. Next, Jacob starts implementing the Pomodoro Technique. He sets a timer for 25 minutes and works on one task during that time without any interruptions. After the timer goes off,* **he takes a five-minute break.***This helps John maintain his focus and avoid burnout. As John continues to implement these changes, he notices a significant improvement in his focus and concentration. He is able to complete tasks more efficiently and with fewer mistakes. He also feels less stressed and more in control of his workload. In conclusion, Jacob was able to enhance his focus and concentration by minimizing distractions, incorporating mindfulness practices, and implementing the Pomodoro Technique. By making these changes, he was able to* *improve his productivity,reduce stress, and achieve his desired outcomes.*

Optimizing Your Workspace

Optimizing your workspace is essential for increased productivity and comfort. By creating an environment that supports your work, you can improve your focus, reduce distractions, and increase efficiency. There are many ways to optimize your workspace, **including decluttering, choosing ergonomic furniture, adjusting lighting, reducing screen time, and personalizing the space.**By following these tips, you can create a workspace that supports your work and helps you achieve your goals.

Optimizing your workspace can help increase productivity and comfort.Here are some tips to help optimize your workspace

Declutter : Keep your workspace free of clutter and only keep the essentials within reach.

Choose Ergonomic Furniture : Invest in comfortable, ergonomic furniture such as a chair and desk that support good posture and reduce strain on the body.

Adjust Lighting : Ensure that your workspace has good lighting, including natural light if possible, to reduce eye strain and improve mood.

Use A Comfortable And Quiet Workspace: Create a workspace that is quiet, well-ventilated, and free of distractions.

Personalize Your Workspace : Add personal touches, such as plants or pictures, to make your workspace feel welcoming and more personal.

Keep Tools And Supplies Within Reach : Keep frequently used tools and supplies within easy reach to reduce the need for

unnecessary movements and distractions.

Reduce Screen Time : Reduce screen time by taking breaks and using anti-glare screens to prevent eye strain and headaches.

By following these tips, you can optimize your workspace, increase your productivity and comfort, and enjoy a more pleasant and efficient work environment.

Lets's Understand The Power of Optimizing Workspace With This Story

Joseph had always struggled with staying focused and productive at work. Despite his best efforts, he found himself **constantly distracted and unable to complete his tasks on time.***After speaking with a coworker, he learned about the importance of optimizing his workspace. Determined to improve his productivity, Joseph decided to take the necessary steps to optimize his workspace. He started by decluttering his desk and only keeping the essentials within reach. He then invested in an ergonomic chair and desk that* **supported good posture and reduced strain on his body.***Next, Joseph adjusted the lighting in his workspace, ensuring that it was well-lit and free of glare. He also created a quiet and comfortable environment by using sound-absorbing materials and keeping his workspace free of distractions.To further personalize his workspace, Joseph added some plants and pictures to make the space feel more welcoming, inspiring and personalized. He also made sure that his tools and supplies were always within reach,* **reducing the need for unnecessary movements and**

distractions. *Finally, Joseph made a conscious effort to reduce his screen time by taking regular breaks and using anti-glare screens to prevent eye strain and headaches.As a result of these changes, Joseph found that* **he was able to focus and be more productive at work.***He was no longer easily distracted and was able to complete his tasks in a timely manner. He was grateful for the lessons he learned about optimizing his workspace and was happy to have created a space that supported his work and helped him achieve his goals.*

Power of Staying On Track

Staying on track refers to the ability to remain focused and committed to achieving a specific goal or set of goals. The power of staying on track lies in the positive outcomes that come from staying focused and motivated. By avoiding distractions, setting achievable milestones, and regularly reassessing progress, **you can increase your chances of success and experience greater satisfaction from reaching your goals**. Additionally, staying on track helps build self-discipline and fosters a sense of accomplishment, which can lead to **increased confidence and motivation for future endeavors.**

Moreover, staying on track can also help in **managing time effectively and reducing stress levels.**When you have a clear plan and stick to it, you are able to prioritize tasks and avoid procrastination, leading to more productive use of time. Additionally, by staying focused and avoiding distractions, you are less **likely to feel overwhelmed and stressed**, leading to a more balanced and fulfilling life. In conclusion, staying on track is a valuable skill that can help individuals achieve their goals, improve productivity, and lead a more fulfilling life.

Common let's understand with Shazia's story

Shazia is a recent college graduate who has just landed her dream job in marketing. She is eager to make a good impression and wants to excel in her role. She sets clear and specific career goals for herself and creates a plan of action to achieve them. Every morning, she starts her day by reviewing her to-do list and prioritizing tasks based on their importance and deadline. She stays focused on her work and avoids distractions, such as checking social media or getting caught up in office gossip. Over the next few months, Shazia's hard work and dedication pay off. She is able to successfully complete multiple projects and is recognized for her contributions by her team and managers. She continues to stay on track and make steady progress towards her career goals. As she sees her progress, her confidence grows and she becomes more motivated to keep pushing forward. Eventually, Shazia is offered a promotion and becomes a team lead. She is **proud of her achievements and grateful for the power of staying on track**. *By sticking to her plan and staying focused on her goals, she was able to achieve her desired outcomes and reach new heights in her career.*

In conclusion, the power of staying on track lies in its ability to help individuals achieve their **desired outcomes, increase productivity, and lead a more fulfilling life.**By setting clear goals and creating a plan of action, staying focused and avoiding distractions, and managing time effectively, individuals can make steady progress towards their aspirations. Whether it's in their personal or professional lives, the ability to stay on track can have a **significant impact on success and satisfaction.**By embracing this skill and incorporating it into their daily routine, individuals can *unlock their full potential and reach new heights.*

Conclusion

Embracing Growth And Continuous Learning

It is a mindset that recognizes the importance of personal and professional development and is committed to continuously acquiring new knowledge and skills. By embracing this mindset, individuals and organizations **can stay ahead of the curve, adapt to change, and achieve their goals.**

Here are some ways to embrace growth and continuous learning:

Set Learning Goals: Identify areas where you want to improve and set achievable learning goals. This can help keep you focused and motivated.

Seek Out New Experiences: Trying new things and exposing yourself to new experiences can help you learn and grow.

Seek Feedback: Ask for feedback from others and be open to constructive criticism. This can help you identify areas for improvement and make progress.

Take Genuine Courses And Attend Great Workshops: Invest in your personal and professional development by taking courses and attending workshops that align with your learning goals.

Read And Stay Informed: Stay informed about your industry and the latest trends by reading articles, books, and attending events.

Network With Others: Network with others in your field and seek out mentorship opportunities. This can help you gain new perspectives and insights.

Embrace Failure: Embrace failure as an opportunity to learn and grow. Don't be afraid to make mistakes and learn from them.

By embracing growth and continuous learning, individuals and organizations can remain competitive, innovate, and achieve their desired outcomes. This mindset can help create a culture of continuous improvement and drive success in all areas of life.

In conclusion, the untold power of productivity lies in the ability to **use one's time and resources**effectively to achieve desired outcomes. By staying focused on goals, prioritizing tasks, and avoiding distractions, individuals can **tap into this power and experience**the benefits of increased efficiency and effectiveness. Whether it's in the **workplace or in one's personal life, the ability to manage time and resources effectively**can lead to greater success, satisfaction, and well-being. The journey to becoming more productive may require some effort and discipline, but the rewards are well worth it. By embracing the untold power of productivity, we can **unlock our full potential and achieve**more than we ever thought

possible. By embracing productivity, individuals and organizations can streamline their processes, increase efficiency, and achieve more in less time. The benefits of productivity are not just limited to the workplace, but extend to all aspects of life, allowing us to spend more time on the things that matter most. Whether it's personal development, relationships, hobbies, or making a positive impact on the world, the power of productivity provides the ***means to make these aspirations a reality.***Embracing productivity is an investment in one's future and the key to unlocking a life of abundance, fulfillment,
and purpose.

The untold power of productivity is a valuable tool for anyone looking to improve their effectiveness and achieve their goals. By mastering the skills of time **management, goal-setting, and focus, individuals can harness this power and experience the benefits of increased efficiency, satisfaction, and success.**Productivity is not just about working harder, but about working smarter and making the most of every moment. The journey to becoming more productive **may be challenging, but the rewards are immeasurable.**So embrace the untold ***power of productivity and discover***what you can accomplish when you make the most of every day.

"The true power of productivity lies in its ability to unlock potential and enhance our ability to achieve our goals, transforming dreams into realities."

9 789356 674639